A **YOU CAN**...EMPOWERMENT SERIES

I0142541

YOU CAN

HEAR FROM GOD

drsherillchong!!!

Cover Design: Dale Sewell

ISBN: 978-976-96192-7-2

ISSN: 0799-5977

All Scripture quotes are followed by the reference and the version or translation that the scripture comes from. All other biblical concepts, principles and ideas, are not representations of any translation, but are presented as they were impressed on my mind at the time of writing:

Published by: The Publisher's Notebook Ltd
Email: thepublishersnotebook@gmail.com
Website: http://thepublishersnotebook.com

THE PUBLISHER'S
NOTEBOOK LIMITED
"ENVISION IT. WE'LL PUBLISH IT"

DEDICATION

I thank God, the Father for giving me Abundant Life. I thank God, the Son for providing The Way to access the Abundant Life; and I thank God, the Holy Spirit for momently leading me into All Truth... and that they are ONE.

I thank my Lord for every person I have interacted with, and every situation I have faced and for how He (God), has used each one to chip away the crusty facades, sandpaper the spines and barbs, and provide opportunity to share God's incredible love on my journey so far.

I thank my mother Linnette Louise Lake-Case, my Dad, Charles Olivier Case, my siblings Joyce Case-Wright, Paulette Bellamy and Donovan Case; Laurel E. Baillie, Earl Constantine Chong and each individual that I interacted with, at any level from the following groups:

Deanery Avenue Case-Webb Crew, Maranatha Gospel Hall, Summerdale Prep. Vaz Preparatory School, Vineyard Town Morning Walk Crew, Delhi Lyons School of Dance, Rowe Studio of Dance, Eddy Thomas, Ivy Baxter, Alma Mock Yen and Jamaica School of Dance., Excelsior High School, Carberry House and the Gymnastic, Dance and Drama clubs; Teen Time Camp, Galilee Gospel Hall, Duff's Business College, The Gospel Medley, The Maranatha Affair, Duff's Fashion Academy, Bethel Evening Bible School (Brethren); La Salle Extension University, *PULSE Ltd,* Merck, Sharpe & Dohme Caribbean, Plyber Company Limited, Scotiabank Jamaica, Jamaica Institute of Management, Mavisville Preparatory School, Jamaica School of Music, Ultramod Limited (Furniture & Fixtures); Jamaica Industrial Development Corporation; Creative House Ltd., Church on the Rock, COTR Dance Ministry, Sonshine Ministries, National Housing Corporation, Allied Business Consultants, Lake, Case & Baillie; Sonshine Manufacturing, Philadelphia Gospel Assembly, Central Christian University, Midlands Bible Institute, Earl's Juice Gardens, Earl & Sherrill Chong Health Ministries, Holiness Christian Church,

Destiny Performing Arts Company, Swallowfield Chapel, Open Heavens HCC, Glory of Zion International.

These have been my family at one time or another; and I still draw love and inspiration from the persons and experiences that enriched my life. From the bad times, I can remember being enveloped by God's arms as I learned wisdom from those experiences. From the good times, I treasure and build on those loving interactions as we move toward common goals.

I love you ALL, and appreciate the contribution that you made to making me who I am today... and the process continues... Thank you, Thank you, Thank You!!!

The material is organized under three areas.

Communication – means of passing on information.

Process – some ways in which I have walked through and processed the information communicated.

Purpose – some of God's intent end results for creating you and me.

Table of Contents

FOREWORD

It is commendable that Dr. Sherrill Chong is putting these things to print and making it available to people because there are a lot of things that she has to say. First of all, I want to look at it in terms of why a person would read this book. I think:

There is a certain amount of pleasure to be derived, in other words, it is delightful, it is interesting, and it has intrinsic value as you read it.

As you read it, you will understand that it has devotional value. Devotional in that it is concerned about the practical relationship people have with God. She is aware that a lot of people have a sort of disjointed experience of church and life; so in the absence of a spiritual director, a person could derive spiritual direction from it.

The author comes to the task **from a breath of knowledge of a lot of things**. Sherrill even has opinions

about how the genes behave. She is deeply schooled in scripture, (pursued a PhD in Biblical Hermeneutics and Jewish Studies); and studied in areas as unrelated as Fashion Designing, Financial Management and Neuroscience.

She comes to it **as an example**, of the health, wealth, peace, love, and joy that comes from a close relationship with her Lord, which she shares with whosoever, wants to partake. One at least has to listen.

It teaches. It is didactic. There are things you will know that you did not know before, if you read this book.

If it is Sherrill's book there are going to be ideas that will confront you, challenge you, or that you have to argue with. It is didactic in the sense that it is challenging you to think because that is Sherrill's approach to life – No one, especially her pastor, and I have been her pastor, is going to push anything down her throat and tell her to swallow. In fact, her temperament is, she is likely to dismiss you with a certain disdain if you are a "Yes" Person. The love of her life was this sort of iconic "No" person. Nobody, not even Sherrill could convince Earl

Chong to do what he didn't want to do. He was her great love until death parted them. There is something she admires in a person who rebels. Therefore, this book is not intended to be some kind of brain washing manual, it is expected for people to think and to respond and to grow. To grow, one has to question, and be willing to be questioned.

So I would say that I envy Sherrill in the sense that she has taken note that nobody is beyond question. At five years old, Sherrill questioned God about whether he was "color-prejudiced". If she at five believes that God can be questioned, then go ahead and ask God the tough questions, and be assured that He will answer because YOU CAN... Hear From God!!!

Rev Dr Sam Vassel - Senior Pastor of the Bronx Bethany Church of the Nazarene, New York,

INTRODUCTION

I have always been a writer and note taker ever since I can remember. My concept is: If it is noteworthy, it is worth making a note! Additionally," Do it now" was another of my mantras, for to me, delayed obedience is disobedience. As a result of these beliefs, I acted immediately on everything I thought was a prompting of the Spirit.

If I was sitting in church listening to a stirring sermon and an idea for a new design flashed across my mind, I immediately transformed my bulletin into my sketch pad and the most innovative house plans, room plans, garden designs, clothing and fashion items, accessories, course and book outlines, are recorded in every conceivable blank square centimeter, with appropriate numbering of steps, developmental sequences and organic note taking. I will share some of the latter in their original

form, at another time, so that you can benefit from that recording method.

At times, I am hit with a flash driving home late, late at night or early in the morning. The next street light becomes my stopping point, and my speed-writing skills are brought into play as I alert my guardian angels to be on the look out for possible predators. At other times when I am cautioned not to stop, I simply slow down, direct my knees to take over the steering wheel and without taking my eyes from the road, pull out my ever present scratch pad and scrawl whatever comes to mind.

All these are taken home and filed under the appropriate category to first enrich my life and then share with anyone wanting to add a new dimension to the wonderful ABUNDANT LIFE Christ died to shower each and every one of us with.

A visit to my home or office, is often an intriguing event as you wonder about the stories behind all these ever changing posters, scribblings and designs…?! These are merely my own reminders, for the present season; which

everyone who is allowed to enter my home is invited to read, adjust, apply or share… or just ignore.

My desire is to help somebody as I negotiate my own path, so that my living is not in vain. May I invite you to trot along with me?

the ALWAYS BLESSED AND HIGHLY FAVORED, sherrill elisabeth lake-case-baillie-chong!!!

COMMUNICATION

CONVERSATION

A dear friend forwarded me this story that was circling on the internet, sometime in 2014. I share this piece first because it so impacted my life at a time when I was belly-aching about things not running smoothly. Hope it will help you too and encourage you to have more conversations with God.

This is the beginning of the email.

Awesome Conversation between God and a man. Read it and don't forget to share it with your friends. GOD BLESS!!!

Man: God, can I ask You a question?

God: Sure

Man: Promise You won't get mad …

God: I promise

Man: Why did You let so much stuff happen to me today?

God: What do u mean?

Man: Well, I woke up late

God: Yes

Man: My car took forever to start

God: Okay

Man: at lunch they made my sandwich wrong & I had to wait

God: Huummm

Man: On the way home, my phone went DEAD, just as I picked up a call

God: All right

Man: And on top of it all, when I got home I just wanted to soak my feet in my new foot massager & relax. BUT it wouldn't work!!! Nothing went right today! Why did You do that?

God: Let me see, the death angel was at your bed this morning & I had to send one of My Angels to battle him for your life. I let you sleep through that.

Man (humbled): OH

GOD: I didn't let your car start because there was a drunk driver on your route that would have hit you if you were on the road.

Man: (ashamed)

God: The first person who made your sandwich today was sick & I didn't want you to catch what they have, I knew you couldn't afford to miss work.

Man (embarrassed): Okay

God: Your phone went dead because the person that was calling was going to give false witness about what you said on that call, I didn't even let you talk to them so you would be covered.

Man (softly): I see God

God: Oh and that foot massager, it had a shortage that was going to throw out all of the power in

your house tonight. I didn't think you wanted to be in the dark.

Man: I'm Sorry God

God: Don't be sorry, just learn to Trust Me…. in All things , the good & the bad

Man: I will trust You

God: And don't doubt that My plan for your day is Always Better than your plan.

Man: I won't God. And let me just tell you God, Thank You for Everything today.

God: You're welcome child. It was just another day being your God and looking after My Children…

PS: I am sorry to disturb you ! My name is God. You hardly have time for me. I love you and always bless you. I am always with you. I need you to spend 30 mins of your time with Me today. Don't pray. Just chat.

Share this if you think it will help someone else.

This is the end of the email.

HEARING FROM GOD

My Perspective Based On God's Word and How I Experienced it.

Every person created has conversations with God starting at conception. Our Creator formed each of us in our mother's womb by speaking to our molecules and cells to come into alignment according to His perfect will. For approximately nine months, God and baby continue this conversation until our Creator has completed the foundational formation and now hands us into the care of our earthly parents who He has given everything needed to continue the job. Well, that's the original plan, at least.

While God is speaking His DNA into the unborn child, the contributing and host parents have the opportunity of agreeing with God to replace the negative aspects of their human DNA with God's; or, allow or reinforce their own DNA during this stage of development. Enter all birth "defects"!!!

The conversation has continued throughout my life to date – 69 years later. At age 5 or 6, I made the decision to agree with, repeat and obey whatever I heard God say. I found that every time I did this, I reaped the benefit of:

❖ **Increased Health** - I was a very sickly child up until age 10. Had deformed feet and had to wear boots with steel in them when all the other little girls were wearing strap shoes and frilly socks. I had mumps, measles, chicken pox, whooping cough, scarlet fever, bronchitis, pneumonia, tonsillitis, adenoids, as well as frequent yearly bouts of influenza, colds and fever, and just feeling sick! My most prominent memory was the visit of our German doctor - Dr. Stamp to our home and his request for me to, "longs out zee tongue" so he could check my throat.

I always received healing from each malady, and miraculously at 10 years, I entered high school, healthy, strong and had no further health challenges. God granted me favour as a champion gymnast, dancer and dramatist. I did fairly well in the

scholastic area, well enough to be offered a teacher's scholarship to UWI – which I did not take up.

❖ **Increased Provision** - I always felt that I had more things than those around me, more favour, more opportunities, more gifts, more talent, more invitations to be part of whatever was happening. I thought we were wealthy, because my parents were always giving away stuff to everyone, and so we as children all followed suit.

❖ **Increased Calm** - I had my fair share of childhood incidents which I considered traumas, but faced them all with relative calm bordering on stubborn stoicism, which I considered to be a blessing at the time.

❖ **Improved Relationships** – Struggling with low self-esteem as a result of cruel comparisons which are a part of interaction with children, I was constantly aware of God's voice telling me that I had value and was loved. I learned to BE who I felt I was, because of God's gift of a mother who never

compared her children, but affirmed each one for who they were. This led to charting my own path and encouraging others to do the same. This did not go down too well in the autocratic school system of the time, nor the 'shut-up and obey' attitude of most churches.

❖ **Increased Joy** - as I learned to turn my constant whining about perceived discrimination because I was the youngest one, into giggling and laughter when I got my own way; or things turned out in my favour. This was my childlike faith. However, this was not always the case. As time went by, I vacillated between accepting what God said and accepting what I heard others say; between what God wanted for me and what I desired for myself; between what God said and what seemed possible; between what God said and what had happened in the past; but I was always aware of His voice – even when I was defiant and disobedient.

In this first introductory volume, I share a few of my scribblings, chosen because of their relevance to my current challenges over the past 3 years, and their ability to buoy me up and keep me afloat.

WHERE ARE YOUR DOWNLOADS COMING FROM???

All DOWNLOADS come from the SPIRITUAL realm and manifest as THOUGHTS which then are communicated to our EMOTIONS and RELATIONSHIPS through the senses of SIGHT, SOUND, SMELL, TASTE and TOUCH. (Expanded in other scribblings.)

All of the above are INPUTS which are responded to in one of three ways in every case. They are ACCEPTED, REJECTED or "IGNORED". This initial RESPONSE will then be amplified to form MOTIVES and ATTITUDES; and then TRANSMITTED into WORDS, and ACTIONS.

Since all that is such a mouthful, let us define what is meant by each of the words that have been capitalized above so that we end up on the same page of understanding which makes it easier to move the concepts from INFORMATION to KNOWLEDGE. (Information to me means a series of facts, while Knowledge means the

understanding of the facts, having applied them and having seen the results.

DEFINITIONS!!!

!!! or ??? : Wherever these appear, the foregoing statement or question is applicable to Spirit, Soul and Body

DOWNLOADS:

Revelations from God - not based on human knowledge.

SPIRITUAL:

Relating to the spirit realm (may include good and evil)

THOUGHTS:

An awareness of an idea or concept from your memory bank

EMOTIONS:

Awareness and or feeling of excited mental state in relationship with oneself (sometimes projected unto others).

RELATIONSHIPS:

The connection, correspondence, contrast or feeling one has with another person, thing or entity.

SIGHT, SOUND, SMELL, TASTE, TOUCH:

Our senses through which we receive, process and transmit information.

INPUTS:

What comes into our spirit-man.

RESPONSE:

What we do or do not do about the inputs.

ACCEPTED:

Willingly received into your spirit, or inner man.

REJECTED:

Blocked from entering, or ejected from remaining in the spirit.

"IGNORED":

A form of passive admission or acceptance into the spirit man.

MOTIVES:

What impels a person to action; eg: fear or love.

ATTITUDES:

Posture and behavior that expresses a way of thinking.

TRANSMITTED:

Passed on, conveyed, communicated

WORDS:

The creative force which starts the process of bringing things into being.

ACTIONS:

The involuntary employment of body parts to carry out a preconceived series of movements intended to achieve a predetermined outcome.

INFORMATION:

The perceived facts about a person, place, thing or entity.

KNOWLEDGE:

The facts gained from experiential involvement.

Well!!! Having soared through those definitions let's get to the CORE OR CENTRE of the question. CORE OR CENTRE being the point or place from which everything emanates. The reason I am so hung up on definitions is that each person has slightly different understanding and interpretations of any given word based on all the factors that make her/him unique.

So, back to the original question of where are you getting your downloads from. Having established that the spiritual realm is that supernatural power that impacts the spirit of man within him to reflect that image; it is our responses or outputs that will determine which SUPERNATURAL power or force we have accepted.

There is a biblical/scientific/philosophical concept that our earth (globe) and its immediate ATMOSPHERE is surrounded by a powerful magnetic field which responds to the energy field in the centre of the earth. This atmosphere is controlled, maintained, or changed by the human

inhabitants and life forms on the earth by the energy waves we receive and send out through our senses.

So, we now have an energy field in the centre, surrounded by the physical structure of the earth which has lifeforms on its surface, surrounded by the atmosphere we are responsible for.

The concept continues that surrounding this atmosphere was the space inhabited by our loving benevolent supernatural creator who created us to reflect His perfect Image. This place/space was called THE HEAVENS. Some TIME back there was a rebellion in The Heavens, where one of the messengers wanted to become the one who sends the message. And so, along with his followers, they were kicked out and fell into the lower part of The Heavens where they inhabit until this day. So that gave rise to the idea that we now have three distinct heavens.

The FIRST HEAVEN – The one controlled by humans; the one we see when we look up; The SECOND HEAVEN - The next concentric band around the earth's immediate atmosphere where the fallen messengers operate

from; and then the THIRD HEAVEN where our creator and His myriads of loyal messengers reside and operate from. (This concept does not in any way alter the truth that God is omnipresent)

So which heaven are your downloads coming from?

The First Heaven? - where all ideas are limited by the confines of time, space and available resources?

The Second Heaven? Where all thoughts and intents are focused on distracting us from God's original intent for us; or

The Third Heaven? Where we are constantly fed with empowering ideas that will develop and hone created beings into the very image of our creator God.

I always have a choice, and in fact, I constantly make a choice, whether by omission or commission.

So where are you getting your downloads from? It is easy to differentiate among the sources, by asking three questions.

1. Is it limited by my senses, capabilities, and present resources?

If the answer is yes, this indicates your downloads are coming from the first heaven.

2. Is it distracting me from God's original plan for my life?

   If the answer to this is yes, this indicates that the download is from the second heaven.

3. Is it reinforcing God's best for me and offering supernatural assistance in ensuring spectacular results?

   This download is from the Third Heaven.

   Where are you getting your downloads???

   What is God saying to YOU now?

COMMUNICATION CLARITY!!!

Most misunderstanding between human beings result from the different meanings or interpretations which each person attaches to words. Isn't it comforting to know that God understands exactly what we mean, because He does not only hear our words but He judges the intents of our hearts.

Because my method of communication is specific and unique to me I will define the words and phrases I use and what they mean to me.

PURPOSE:

The original intent of an item as designed by the creator of that item.

FIVE ELEMENTS OF LIFE:

Fresh Air, Pure Water, Sunlight, Earth Foods & PEMF's (Pulsed Electro Magnetic Fields)

FIVE SENSES:

Sight, Sound, Smell, Taste and Touch.

ABUNDANT LIFE:

Excesses in Health, Wealth, Peace, Love and Joy used to meet my own needs first, then to share with all those who wish to accept this gift from my overflow.

THE 3-7-12 WAY:

An approach to life and lifestyle practices accepting the three main trinities of life: Father, Son and Holy Spirit (one); spirit, soul and body of humans (one); The heavens, the earth and hell, the three dimensions of the past, present and future domiciles of man.

These are only three of the many, many triangles of life which mirror the indivisible nature of God; for God is one, not three but one.

SH'MA:

Hear, O Israel, the Lord thy God is one, and thou shall love the Lord with all thy heart, all thy soul and all thy might or strength.

GOD'S CYCLES:

Based on the movement of the heavenly bodies which set God's order for renewal, The Blessing, and empowerment through the yearly feasts; monthly first fruits and God's purposes for each new month; and the weekly Shabbat (Sabbath).

GOD'S LOVE:

Demonstrated through John 3:16 (God's Love Gives); Joshua 1:8 (God's Words Work); and Jeremiah 29:11 (God's Plan Succeeds). As my life unfolded, I could always return to this very foundational conversation.

PROCESS

IMPERATIVES!!!

In this segment I include some of the habits that I employed during my journey so far, to keep my ears open. This is not a prescriptive; it is only a descriptive of how I was impressed by the Holy Spirit to adjust my program as preparation for what the enemy had up his sleeve. For God is ALWAYS ahead of our adversary; ALWAYS prepares His children for every danger up ahead; and ALWAYS leads us to the still waters of health, wealth, peace, love, and joy. ... EVERY TIME!

MY CURRENT RITUAL as at April 2016:

This is after my pre-ritual procedures which differ every morning; of recording my dream(s), or not; waking thanksgiving, recognizing and activating my angels (see note below on this); and aligning my spirit with God's Spirit in recognizing the priority of the next 24 hours.

- Pray God's will for all members of the body of Christ and all unsaved.

- Pray Jamaica's National Anthem - both verses!

- Pray the Lord's Prayer with application to myself, my family, my calling or career, my church, my communities, my nation and the world.

- Read the selected passage from the Bible and apply it to myself.

This is the skeleton; and it seems that every morning, there is some change in focus based on some occurrence of the day before or some emphasis that God impresses on me that will change the course of my life ahead.

This activity usually starts at 4.a.m. and takes two to two and a half hours but has on occasions been as short as zero to thirty minutes, and as long as eight hours. It usually starts in my bed as I move from unconscious into sub consciousness and can continue in that location or not;

move to my 'closet', the bathroom, the kitchen, circling the house inside and/or outside, moving into the garden or...

Oh, the bliss of living alone – by the time of publishing, I will be experiencing the bliss of sharing my space...

An imperative that I still grapple with is... getting in to bed by 8 p.m. This is no bliss but I keep telling myself that the rewards are more than worth it.

Note on: recognizing and activating my angels. I have always been aware of the presence of invisible forces assisting and protecting me. Additionally, I have been guided and helped by who I thought were human beings, only to have them simply disappear! So I inquired of the Lord, and started researching the work of angels in the bible. I found out that they were innumerable, powerful messengers from God sent to guide, provide for, protect, deliver, gather, direct activities, comfort, and minister to those who would accept the call of Christ on their lives. They also brought the answers to prayers for individuals, families, communities, nations and regions. They announced God's blessings, and favour on mankind as well as curses and warnings of impending doom on those who would not repent.

Recognizing and accepting their purpose and presence, and requesting their assistance, not only activates them, but cuts the fear and anxiety to zero; because they are holy, wise, meek, obedient and concerned about our welfare. Daily I post them around my home, and whatever I own; around my family, my affairs and activities, communities, nation, leadership of church and state, and deploy them to minister to all those who have a need. No need to worry after that! I am care-free.

It is so comforting to know that there is no miscommunication between God and me. That He understands exactly what I desire even when my attempts are blubbering, inarticulate, or just make absolutely no sense.

It is also a joy to be led by the Holy Spirit to just the right scriptures that bring clarity and assurance, especially when confronted by a frazzled client in the middle of a meltdown.

God is good, all the time!!!

21 CHANGE AGENTS

Do you want to have abundant life in spirit, soul and body? Just engage the following 21 change agents which have a 100% success rate if used in the prescribed proportion. It will take some time and effort, but your results are sure... And if you fail in your efforts, you can always 'fall back ' on No. 21.   IT'S INFALLIBLE !!!

CORRECT & MAINTAIN THE HEALTH OF THE BODY:

1. Fresh Air

2. Pure Water

3. Direct Sun

4. Earth Foods

5. PEMF's (Pulsed Electro Magnetic Fields Or Energy Sources)

The concept of energy is often explained from different perspectives.   In Electricity it is referred to as atoms of frequency, In Chinese medicine it is called Chi or Qui, In chemistry and biology we hear of molecules, but it is the life-force that keeps things together. Everything that exists, resonates with energy, even inanimate objects like steel or paper. With regard to human beings, we have energy pathways which are part of our brain and nervous system. These energy pathways can be blocked by negative emotions like fear, trauma, and unloving actions against God, self and others (called the works of the flesh in the bible). These blocks lead to physical dis-eases, because our life-force is not able to circulate freely. The energy pathways can be cleared and kept clear by the positive emotions like love (called the fruit of the Spirit in the bible). On a physical level energy is depleted in the activities of life and may be replaced and increased by contact with the earth: walking barefooted on the grass or soil, or burying yourself in the sand or soil. Breathing clean air, drinking pure water, getting sufficient sun and eating unprocessed food from the earth, will also replace depleted energy.

CHANGE THE ATMOSPHERE:

(By your acceptance or rejection of what God has deposited in your spirit, and are expressed through the senses of:)

6. Sight

7. Sound

8. Smell

9. Taste

10. Touch

RESUSCITATE FROM NUTRITIONAL DEFICIENCIES: (God's original Plan for maintaining cellular balance given to Adam and Eve in Genesis 1: 29)

11. Fruit

12. Vegetables

13. Nuts/Seeds

14. Peas/Beans

15. Grain

REPAIR ALL CHEMICAL IMBALANCES IN THE SYSTEM:

16. Vitamins

17. Minerals

18. Protein

19. Chlorophyll

20. Enzymes

RESTORE PERFECT HEALTH IN BODY , SOUL, AND SPIRIT, AND RESURRECT ANYTHING DEAD:

21. Love

Having shared twenty-one of the innumerable change agents provided for us by our wonderful, generous heavenly Father, I think it is only fair that I warn you of the one negative change agent which can cancel out the positive effects of all the above. It is the only weapon that the enemy has… and it is **F E A R**!

There is only one thing that human beings fear, and that is: fear of a negative outcome. Fear that what God has promised us, and what He has sent Jesus to provide for us, and what He has sent Holy Spirit to lead us into... will not materialize. This is what caused the first sin, and every other sin committed since that day. Think of it! Satan tempted Eve by telling her that God wanted her to be less than... He wanted to keep her from becoming wise, and then she added to it that God was keeping from her, something that appeared good to eat. Here Eve was operating from the fear of deprivation. Satan made her feel that God wanted to deprive her. She was deceived by Satan and took the bait. Her husband, on the other hand, chose to go along with his wife rather than obey God. A deadly decision which is repeated in so many families to this day.

Would you like to resurrect your faith to the point where all fear has to go? Just use No.21 above; because perfect love casts out (gets rid of, obliterates) all fear. Remember that all fear comes from the enemy; because God has not given you or me or anyone, a spirit of fear, but He has given us the power to love, which produces self-control, or a sound mind.

EXERCISE MANTRA

As far back as I can remember I have been involved in physical exercise of one form or another on a daily basis. Even when I am laid up in bed, immobilized with one illness or another, I would find a routine to do with whatever part of my body could still move. I always tried to do my routines to gospel music or the spoken word, and whenever I was involved in a class using accompanying sounds that were not glorifying God, my voice could be heard above the noise substituting my own words for whatever did not suit me. (My instructors and classmates were not pleased, so I dropped out).

About 20 years ago when I started doing and teaching rebounding, I realized that counting was a very accurate way of keeping track of your sets; and so I asked the Lord for a set of declarations that I could do in multiples of 30 counts... Here it is!

I LOVE the LORD with ALL my HEART, soul, MIND and STRENGTH (6)

I HAVE a-BUN-dant HEALTH (4)

I HAVE a-BUN-dant WEALTH (4)

I HAVE a-BUN-dant PEACE (4)

I HAVE a-BUN-dant LOVE (4)

I HAVE a-BUN-dant JOY (4)

I HAVE a-BUN-dant LIFE! (4)

(Total 30)

After just two minutes of this, my spirit is soaring and the rest of the time just simply disappears as I glide through the rest of my paces – also works well for aerobics, strength training, jogging and power walking. I also use this whenever I am at the public gym, or working with a personal trainer, where their choice of music is not usually to my liking.

GREENS, BEANS AND BERRIES

By now, I am sure you are aware that God speaks to me in Threes, Sevens, and Twelves. That's how I came up with THE 3-7-12 WAY. God always has A WAY – a way up, a way through, a way around and a way out! In THE 3-7-12 WAY I have put together all of the downloads I have received about God's solutions to the challenges that I have faced during my lifetime so far. These principles will also work for future challenges for they are based squarely on the written, spoken, and incarnate Word of God.

Having survived attacks from cancer-2004 & 2006; Pulmonary issues- too numerous to mention; and suppressed anxiety - 1990, 2005, & 2016; I thought I needed a program to lick all three for good.

As usual I got the ultimate solution first: "Think on these things"! Wherever I focused my mind, the spirit and the body must follow. Although the initial impetus enters through the spiritual realm, it is the response of the mind (in thoughts first, then expressed in words.) that will determine the way the body will go. Think about the bad outcome that could take place, and the body immediately is tricked into responding as if it has already happened. Visualize the best possible outcome, and the body starts to beef up its resources to produce this outcome.

But this is just the motivation – Now I need to sink down into my heart, (which is in my belly bottom) and focus in prayer on forgiving God, myself and whoever else comes to mind first. As I receive God's forgiveness which is instantaneous, I stay in that place until I am at peace!!! This is **step one**.

Step two is the action that you need to take to reinforce and maintain the gains made in step one. That's where my download of Greens, Beans & Berries came in. These three categories of food (taken in a whole food form) have been found to be very effective in preventing AND reversing the symptoms of: Depression, Anxiety, Stress, Diabetes, High Blood Pressure, Cancers, Cholesterol, Mucous and Pulmonary (lung-related) Issues.

As usual **Step Three** is the clincher. This has to do with changing my lifestyle and developing a habit. We have all had experiences of how we have allowed our minds to lead us down the wrong path, and how we have allowed our thoughts to lift us out of harm's way. We all have had experiences of how our abstention from or imbibing of certain substances have resulted in ill-health or improved vitality. In order to successfully complete Step Three, I need to do three things:

1. Visualize it;

2. Record it (write it down); and

3. Daily do something that will advance the process.

So here I am again, choosing to take another giant step forward, by writing out another "Time Investment Plan" for the next three months, to incorporate more thinking on those things that I love having in my life; taking those actions that are in my best long-term interest, and choosing to love the life I live, in order to live the life I love 24/7 !!!

GUIDELINES!!!

Most of us have heard the phrase: "There are many ways to skin a cat"; or "You can take several routes to reach your destination". These are factual statements! Using the second phrase, you could use five amazingly interesting routes to get from Kingston to the North Coast:

1) West along the South Coast route, through St. Elizabeth to Negril;

2) East along the south coast through St. Thomas to Portland;

3) North, through the mountains using the Junction Road to St. Mary;

4) North using the old road through Spanish Town, Bog walk, Moneague, to Discovery Bay; or

5) North on the highway from Kingston, ending in St. Ann.

I have used all five routes in the past and achieved my objectives; HOWEVER, each time my goal or objective was slightly different.

Because Life is a continuum, and we are always changing; our guidelines will sometimes need to be tweaked - but in which direction? Only the person who is clear on the end results desired, can make the adjustment required, to hit the target bulls eye. Only the person who has the big picture (God) can position the different players with precision.

So, regardless of my knowledge, foresight and plans, I cannot afford to lean to my own understanding. Whichever way I planned to take, whatever path I intended to trod, I simply submit them to His scrutiny for His directions. It is in these times that I have marveled at the "all things that worked together for my good"!

Needless to say, this is not always my experience; and when it is not, I simply trace back my steps to see which guidelines I chose not to take or just simply ignored. God has made great plans for me. He has plotted out an exciting journey leading to my ending in a blaze of glory. If I really believe this, I have the wonderful opportunity of acquainting myself with His plans daily; following closely in His footsteps along the journey; and enjoying the ride.

THE FALL!!!

Read Genesis 2:15-17 and Genesis 3:1-7

ALL FALLS ARE THE RESULT OF OUR CHOOSING TO EAT OF THE FRUIT OF THE TREE OF THE KNOWLEDGE OF GOOD AND EVIL.

Before the fall, man only knew good. He was in the state of innocence. God communicated with man spirit to spirit. From day one, God made Adam and Eve know that every action has consequences. God said that if Adam and Eve ate of the tree of the knowledge of good and evil, they would die. When Adam chose to eat of the prohibited tree, the consequence for Him and all His offspring was death. I think that the word death, does not mean annihilation but it means separation. In this instance, their spirits became dead to (separated from) God. So instead of having revelation knowledge from God's Spirit to their spirit, they now had to use their limited senses to evaluate information, and to make decisions.

The knowledge of good and evil gave opportunity for the curse. For without the knowledge of evil, we have no options from which to choose! Now that mankind had become aware of both good and evil, when faced with every decision a choice has to be made between the two. Choose the good and be blessed; or choose the evil and be cursed.

As persons who have experienced the new birth and have chosen the path of following Jesus, we still have the same choice, to heed God's admonition, "of the tree of the knowledge of good and evil, thou shall not eat..." God did not say we were not to be aware of it, but we were not to eat of it, (or engage our senses in taking it into our spirits). This means not to focus on this knowledge with our sight, nor our hearing, nor our sense of smell, nor our taste, nor our sense or touch or feeling; not to study it, and not to teach it to others. Because this new knowledge was based

47

on the reasoning of our five senses, it is limited to conclusions based on logic and reason. The new birth means that our spirits are reborn and are no longer dead or separated from God's Spirit. The spirit to Spirit communication is reinstated.

If God has given me everything I need to live an abundant and Godly life, and the power of the Holy Spirit to maintain and sustain my witness; why do I fall so often? Since I have been given the power of choice, I do not have to do what God has said. I fall because I choose to lean to my own understanding instead of acknowledging God in all my ways. His way is to submit to Holy Spirit; resist the enemy, and he will flee from me.

Nothing is wrong with questioning God's ways, or asking for help, or not understanding His ways. I just need to know that He is my Father, and I am His child, Jesus is my big brother, and I shall receive all the mothering I need from Holy Spirit. I can trust His ways. He only wants to reinforce the knowledge of Good in my life, and give me the power to follow it.

The enemy's plan is to bring division, hate and chaos in families. This will only happen when we revert to and accept our knowledge of evil and choose to walk that path instead of the good or right way that we know. All human beings since Adam and Eve's fall, are born with the knowledge of good and evil. We instinctively know what is good and what is evil. However, there is a diabolical pull it seems toward evil instead of good. It's the same old plan of the enemy which has become a genetic predisposition inherited from Adam and Eve.

God has restored the spirit to Spirit communication. He wants to restore the family and relationships within the family, communities and nations which will only come by following the knowledge of good (or God).

Get to know and follow God.

PRAYER & RESTORATION - PSALM 51

The objective of most of my prayers is for forgiveness and restoration of my peace. For whenever I am troubled, frustrated or even just disappointed, I know that a door, or even a crack in the door, has been opened by me. That's why I love the stories in the bible which show man's failings and God's response of restoration when we ask for forgiveness.

I share a few instances below:

Content: Prayer as a result of the Word of God through the prophet Nathan in Samuel after David's sin with Bathsheba

Gal. 6 - If a brother is overtaken in a fault those who are spiritual shall confront him in such a way that he is restored considering your own frailty.

Goal: Immediate restoration to fellowship with God and fellowship of believers; and eventual restoration to leadership, if he qualifies.

Another story comes to mind. There were two women who had recently given birth to babies. During the night, one rolled over her child resulting in the death of the infant. This mother promptly switched her dead child with the baby of the other woman, and then claimed the baby who was alive as her own.

When brought before King Solomon as the judge, He ruled that the live baby be cut in half and shared between the two women. The woman who was not the mother of the live baby agreed that this would be just, but the real mother preferred to give up her child, to keep him alive. The live child was restored to his mother.

A most significant feature of this story is that there is no record of the mother who switched the babies, receiving punishment. Behold, your sin shall find you out.

The purpose of God's Justice is to protect life and demonstrate His unconditional love for all... both the victim and the perpetuator of the crime.

Spurgeon says: Seat him in the back pew until his good deed override the notoriety of his sin.

Some church tradition says: Let him feel the full extent of the law, then apply church discipline. God says that His grace is sufficient for me, and that I can rely on and appropriate His strength when I am weak!

Whose justice do you prefer???

PRAYER (key to a great and growing relationship with God) Daniel 9

- Communication – The lack of good communication, causes all dysfunctions in relationships; good communication will result in growing and giving relationships.

- There are differences in communication styles between men and women, but God understands them all.

  Men can only do one thing at a time so they listen, then speak.

  Women communicate and multitask, so they talk back and forth appearing not to listen, but they hear and answer back.

- Communication with God: Requires that we listen to him first, (from scripture or prophesy) then ask for His mind to understand before we engage in prayer. I do not need to remind him of what has gone wrong, just what he has promised to do to make it right.

- Prayer must be <u>theologically</u> informed. We must know the mind and heart of God first (prophecy of Jeremiah). We must give our full attention to what God is saying.

- Jeremiah 25 "The word came, but they have not listened," but 70 years later, after their enemies had oppressed them, they were ready to listen, only then could they receive God's blessing.

- 2nd Timothy 2:7 <u>Reflect</u> on what God is saying and he will give full revelation; and understanding the word of prophecy that comes from an anointed servant of God, must also be reflected on and applied to my life. Be like the Bereans: They searched the scriptures to see if what the apostles said was true. This is also a prerequisite for prayer.

- Persons engaging in prayer must be <u>socially alert</u> to discern the times and seasons. (This information does not have to come from the media, it can come from direct revelation from God.)

Ear to the ground, and heart in heaven, (seated in heavenly places).

I understand from the Scripture, I turn to the Lord and I confess it in prayer!

Look at the prayers of David. How did David communicate with God?

❖ All relationships are based on healthy conversation, listening and contemplation. Do this process and then speak.

Look at the prayer of Daniel. Notice how Daniel communicated through images. He saw, he held the image, and he chose to act on what he had seen.

Each of us communicate a little differently, with God, with ourselves and with others, and so we should because God has made us all different... unique. So however you communicate know that God understands exactly where you are, what you feel, and what you need; and is ready, willing and able to supply the solution.

VISUALIZATION

When you hold the image of your goal on the screen of your mind in the present tense, you are agreeing or in harmony with God's intent for you, when he placed that vision or dream in your heart.

Co-operate with God and bring His plans for your life, to pass.

By focusing on that image, you are attracting like energy of similar activities to combine with and enhance what you are focused on. Overcome fear of man or what others think.

❖ The Lord is my helper; I will not fear what man shall do, think or speak to me; or be seized by alarm. (see Heb.13:6)

❖ Let God be true and every man a liar. That thou might be justified in thy sayings and might overcome when thou art judged! (see Rom. 3:14)

❖ I will praise thee for I am fearfully and wonderfully made, marvelous are thy works and that my inner self knows right well. (see Ps.139:14)

Remember that God encourages us to pull down every imagination, every thought that is not consistent with the best that He wants for us. And to replace it with an imagination that lines up with His thoughts towards us.

SHERRILL CHONG'S TWELVE - (LAWS OF ABUNDANT LIFE)

ITAL LIVITY EXPO

I was invited to present at the subject and as is my custom, I consulted the Lord about going, and what to say. Sometimes I prepare copious notes, rehearse my presentation, then open my mouth and He fills it with totally new material, that I knew absolutely nothing about before uttering it. This was not the case here. He told me how to adapt and add to BOB PROCTOR'S 11, and create a God-Breathed list that ensures a life that matters. Here they are:

1. THINKING – Your thoughts create your life. Choose them well.

2. SUPPLY – There is no lack because nothing diminishes, and God daily loads us with Benefits.

3. ATTRACTION - Whatever you focus on (think about, speak about and visualize); is drawn to you.

4. RECEIVING - Be a gracious receiver, and become a channel of blessing to others.

5. INCREASE - Everything was created to grow and increase daily, Be an active part of this process.

6. COMPENSATION - Return on Investment is always related to how much is invested. Sow a grain of corn, and you will reap hundreds or thousands.

7. NON-RESISTANCE - Whatever you resist, persists. Learn to flow effortlessly with the voice of God's Spirit within you.

8. FORGIVENESS - Forgive and find freedom and peace. Not to forgive is to be at enmity with yourself.

9. SACRIFICE - The more sacrificial the giving, the larger your capacity to receive.

10. OBEDIENCE - Always follow the leading of God's Spirit within, for it leads you into all truth.

11. SUCCESS - You and I were created for a purpose. As I live my purpose, I experience success. (or Shalom –

bringing everything into perfect upright order, where nothing is broken or missing.)

12. LOVE - Giving and receiving Love is the reason we exist. It is the solution to all the challenges of life.

THE DAILY DISCIPLINES OF BLISS

- MEDITATION on God's Words– clears all blockages in our energy pathways, which are our communication channels.

- VISUALIZATION of God's plans – … and see your perfect life unfolding

- INTENTIONAL STUDY – study to show yourself a workman who does not need to be ashamed.

- INSPIRATIONAL READING – Daily read God's word. It will constantly motivate you to the right action.

- GRATITUDE – daily practice of this, maintains correct attitude and raises the happiness level.

- THE GIVING AND RECEIVING OF LOVE

- PRACTICE BECOMES PERFECT or makes one complete….. e v e n t u a l l y !

Each one of us can live an awesome life of abundance, happiness and fulfillment by practicing THE DAILY DISCIPLINES OF BLISS.

Always remember that positive experiences bring HAPPINESS

Personal growth and giving bring FULFILLMENT

WHY WE MUST TURN

God's revelation to us as His creation is progressive. He does not reveal all the steps along the way He has planned to bring us to a prosperous and successful end. He tells us that this is His plan for everyone and everything He created. He then gives us the opportunity to choose to walk in His Way, as He reveals it or not.

As a child, I understood this concept very well because it was taught and modelled in our home by our parents. When anything evil occurred, we were told that it was a result of someone, somewhere in the universe choosing to follow the voice of the enemy instead of the voice of God; AND that whatever the enemy meant for evil, God would turn it around for the good of those who obeyed Him, and use it for the blessing of many.

As I grew, this concept shaped my world view, as I observed world events, our national cultures, and the lifestyles within the church "improve and develop" by accepting more and more ungodly principles, as a route to "success". I was strongly aware that in life there are parallel cultures – Godly and ungodly- and I was always free to choose any one and suffer the consequences or reap the rewards.

So I could understand why 'unbelievers' blamed God for everything that went wrong, but I could never understand why Christians were always blaming the government, the white people, the rich people and the criminals for the things that went wrong in our country. Every prayer meeting in our church was prefaced by: "Prayer changes things"; "Men ought always to pray and not to faint"; - I guess that is why the ladies were not allowed to pray aloud – and, "If my people who are called by My Name would humble themselves and pray, seek my face, and turn from their wicked ways, then will I hear from heaven, I will forgive their sins and heal their land". This last quote clearly places the solution for the healing of our land squarely in the hands of God's People. However, it was always used only as a support for calling times of special prayer.

Recently in Jamaica, my beloved island nation, the 2016 Election was won by the body of Christ humbling ourselves, praying 24/7, and seeking God's face, for a release from the bondage of sickness, poverty, turmoil and war, lovelessness, and a lack of joy. These are all curses that we as a people have accepted and perpetuated. But this is not the end of the story, we all have a choice to engage earthly sorrow which leads to death; or, engage Godly sorrow which leads to repentance and life. Our plea for change has been heard and supernaturally answered. The process of change has started and will be truncated and thwarted until we TURN from our wicked ways. Not the government, nor the criminals, but the people of God, who are called by God's name!!!

This has always been God's prescription for healing and divine health– the healing of the individual, body, soul and spirit; marriages, families, communities, nations, and the body of Christ worldwide. Most importantly, the taking of this prescription – the whole course – is the most effective witness to unbelievers; for as they see the transformation in the lives of those of us who call ourselves believers, they will high-tail it to beg for some of what we have. And what a joy it is to share THE BLESSING that comes from turning, staying turned, and continuing to turn as new things are revealed to us.

My choice is to turn, stay turned, and continue turning. Selah!

What is God saying to YOU?

PURPOSE

WHAT IS MY PURPOSE?

Some questions I asked God, and what I thought He answered.

What Is My Purpose? or Why Was I Created?

Answer: *To be a recipient and channel for God's Love and Glory.*

AND

To embrace the gift of ABUNDANT LIFE in Spirit, Soul and Body.

How Am I To Actualize That Purpose?:

Answer: *By utilizing the FIVE ELEMENTS OF LIFE. (freely given to every human being), through the FIVE SENSES, (also given by God at conception). See 21 Change Agents.*

<u>The Process !!!</u>

This process I call THE 3-7-12 WAY, based on the SH'MA, GOD'S CYCLES, AND GOD'S APPOINTED

FEASTS. Thus saith the Lord, Stand ye in the ways, and see, and ask for the old paths, where is the good way, and walk therein, and ye shall find rest for your souls. Jeremiah 6:16 KJV

3-7-12 WAY (THE) – One approach to a successful Kingdom Lifestyle, based on the SHEMA (Deut.6:4), understanding God's Cycles- (the movement of the heavenly bodies), and His Appointed Feasts.

The 3-7-12 Way

Wouldn't it be great if we could produce the God Vitamin in our bodies; and all other nutrients we need without changing our diets?

Wouldn't it be great if we could change our DNA and all our inherited genetic pre-dispositions, and revert to living the way God created us to live?

Wouldn't it be great if every person on this or that super product reversed every negative health condition in 64 days? ....AND learned how to take total control of their health and their life?

There are millions of us on this planet who have embraced this lifestyle, and are living above the brain-damaging stresses of this time and in fact, using those same stressors as empowering agents as we soar, sail, circumnavigate above and around every challenge to excel, master and manifest our best life through the power of Love.

Wow! That is quite a mouthful, but it feels so great going down; and when it is all digested, it just oozes out of our pores to affect everyone we interact with to reach out and embrace it and start a fire that cannot be contained, that burns up all the dross; and before you know it we emerge like pure Gold!

Enter *THE 3-7-12 WAY* based on God's cycles of renewal and regeneration.

When God gave us the mandate to "Be fruitful and multiply and replenish the earth", He also gave us detailed fool-proof methodologies for accomplishing this.

He showed us how to renew and rebuild our souls and bodies to line up with His Spirit that He has put in us; so that we could actually be expressions of His likeness and image as we live our lives on a daily basis.

PRICELESS - THAT'S WHO I AM

Becoming Priceless !!!

GODDESSES NEVER AGE is a program by Dr. Christiane Northrup, which just popped up in my inbox... how appropriate! As is my normal practice, I enquire of God for His take on this statement. Was I blown away by His answer?! I will put below what I heard Him say to me.

"My daughter, you are indeed a goddess, for you are the daughter of God; and you will never age. As you grow older you will increase in beauty, vitality and value until you become priceless – a treasured jewel, fit for the proposal of the King of Kings. Find and focus on all my promises, keep them in front of your eyes, and speak them day and night. Grow and produce my FRUIT, receive my GIFTS, and share my LOVE with everyone.

Remember my child that getting older is inevitable. Aging is, however, optional. You choose to age and decrease; or mellow and get better and better. Use only those who improved and increased with age, as your role models – like Moses, Joshua and Caleb; all three believed God against all odds. Choose to grow older like a priceless antique which increases in value as it ages. The older it gets the more valuable it becomes. Become more valuable as a tool in My hand, become more valuable as an example of God's power to renew and sustain, and more valuable as a channel and expression of God's love, goodness and glory.

Every day you have a choice of cultures to follow – Mine (God's) or man's. As you face the challenges of life, and your inborn desires; choose to follow only, My solutions, My directives, and My sustainable pleasures.

My desire for you, as you become my priceless treasure is to enjoy: Exalted Emotions (Fruit of the Spirit); Elevated Cognition (Gifts of the Spirit); and Eternal Shalom (Completeness); for you are priceless to me. That is why I desire you as My Bride.".

These were my answers. Yours may be even more amazing, so why don't you seek Him for yourself. And remember that whatever He discloses He will bring to pass.

Note: I am a female son of God as seen in John 3:1; Philippians 2:15, and 1 John 1:12. Christ repeated in John 10:34-36, that we are Gods, as originally written in Psalm 82:6, and Children of the Most High.

What is God saying to YOU?

PERSPECTIVES!!!

Definition: Art of so drawing on a plane surface as to give the effect of solidarity and relative distance and size; apparent relation between visible objects in nature, or as to position, distance, relation or proportion between parts of a subject; vista, view embracing various distances, mental retrospect or prospect. (Oxford Dictionary)

On every idea, thing or entity, there are at least three perspectives: mine, yours, and God's. Each person's perspective is one of the indicators of their purpose.

Every person alive has a different perspective on every issue.   This is because each person is viewing the issue from a different angle, and that angle is influenced by your God given unchangeable TEMPERAMENT; your self-selected PERSONALITY; and your GENETIC PREDISPOSITION + MEMORY... and I think this is just wonderful because that is how God designed and created me to be: UNIQUE (one-of-a-kind), DIFFERENT (from every other person); and CREATIVE (to give rise to or bring into existence).

The challenge is FIRST to embrace, celebrate and engage my own perspective; SECOND, to embrace, celebrate and engage your perspectives, and THIRD, to submit them all to God's perspective. For it is only the omnipresent, omnipotent, omniscient God that sees the whole picture from all sides; present, past and future; the end from the beginning all at one time!

It is only when we submit both our perspectives to God that He can add His perspective to successfully conclude every matter for my benefit, for your benefit, and for the will and purposes of God to come to pass.

In order to be a successful leader in a marriage, a family, at school, at work, at church, in the community, in your chosen field of interest; in your nation or in the world; one MUST be willing and able to address and overcome the three challenges mentioned above, and then be the cohesive agent to synchronize them with God's intent and purpose. For everyone's perspective has value and can be embraced, celebrated and engaged. This is the measure of a great leader; and we are all created to lead (influence) someone else in one area or another.

Of course, my first awareness of this concept came at age 5 or 6 when I asked God if He was colour-prejudiced, His answer to the negative led my mind to wonder how He could embrace every one of his vast and varied creation. I guess He knew exactly why He created us all different, to fulfill a different part of His purpose. From this, I learnt to embrace the differences in everyone I encountered.

Another great leader was my mother Linnette Louise Lake-Case. who always celebrated with equal enthusiasm, the accomplishments of her three biological children, as well as all of her music students, AND the gardener, helpers, milkman, bread man and garbage collectors. She could find something to affirm in all of us, that only a mother could see. This is when I decided I could be myself, regardless of the unkind comments, and rejection from those who hadn't a clue who they were, and therefore could not appreciate the differences in human personality and temperaments.

The third great leader I would like to mention is the Rev. Dr. Sam Vassel, currently Senior Pastor of the Bronx Bethany Church of the Nazarene, New York; whom I had the privilege to be pastored by as a member of Holiness Christian Church, Bethune Avenue, in Kingston Jamaica. I watched him extend the hand of fellowship and engage in ministry, congregants of differing nationalities and faith perspectives, utilizing their gifts and gifting to strengthen and build the Kingdom of God here on earth. Here I saw in practice, a great leader who looked beyond my faults, and saw my need to contribute the best of what I had to offer, to the Lord of Lords and the King of Kings.

Every person made by God was created to lead in one or several arenas or areas of influence. God has surrounded us with all the tools and resources that we need to complete the job successfully. Let us embrace, celebrate and engage the differing perspectives that we interface with for they are God's gifts to complete us individually and collectively as the Body of Christ.

GOD'S SACRED CALENDAR – Leviticus 23

God's Sacred Calendar is based on the movement of the heavenly bodies; i.e. the sun, the moon, the stars; and the impact they make on the earth. This determines the times, and cycles of weeks, months and years which are punctuated by The weekly Sabbath, First fruits and the seven Feasts each year, as reminders of God's past, present and future covenants with His people. Keeping these solemn appointments was our part of the covenant.

By His people I mean the Jewish Nation and the branch that has been engrafted in, of Gentile people who have accepted and embraced Yeshua as their Messiah, Lord, and King.

Why we should celebrate these feasts, and their significance for the end-time church.

SABBATH

We are reminded to keep the Sabbath day each week, resting, free from labour, and dedicated to the Lord.

As we keep this weekly observance, we are reminded that there is a permanent Sabbath's rest for the believer which God wants us to enjoy.

PASSOVER FESTIVAL

Celebrated the 14th day of Nisan (March – April). This annual feast recalled the sacrifice of a lamb in Egypt and the passing over of the death angel. This was immediately followed by the Feast of Unleavened Bread.

UNLEAVENED BREAD

*Held Nisan 15 – 21 (March - April) w*hen the people ate unleavened bread to symbolize the haste with which they left Egypt. Jesus was crucified during the annual Passover observance. The blood of the lamb that had saved the Hebrew people from destruction in Egypt, looked forward to the perfect eternal sacrifice Jesus made for all believers. We now celebrate Him as our Passover lamb, the Lamb of God who takes away the sin of the world.

FIRST FRUITS

Held Nisan 16 (March - April and Sivan 6 May - June) during the Feast of Unleavened Bread and the Feast of Pentecost.

This was an end-of-harvest celebration where a special offering of the first and best of their crops was brought to present to their God. This has been practiced by the Jews since first instituted by God, in recognition of God's blessing and favor which He continuously showers on us.

FEAST OF PENTECOST (HARVEST OR WEEKS)

Started Sivan 6 (May –June) 50 days after the Barley Harvest.

This is a harvest Festival expressing thanksgiving to God for their crops. It was also a time when God's people recognized Him as the Provider of all good things. He was the one who sent the rain, made their crops to flourish, and protected them from harm and danger. Early Christian believers experienced miraculous outpourings of God's Spirit while gathered to observe Pentecost. It was at the yearly gathering after the ascension of Christ that the Holy Spirit was sent. New Testament believers celebrated this time, basically in the same way with great festivities, story-telling and a time to commune with God and receive special revelation. This was the precursor to the Harvest festivals which are still practiced in some denominations today.

TRUMPETS (ROSH HASHANAH)

Held Tishri 1, 2 (Sept – Oct.)

Characterized by the blowing of trumpets and rams' horns, it was believed to have been held to counteract the influence of Babylon's New Year's festival. Started while Israel was in captivity. It is now celebrated as a time to hear God's voice in the midst of a world listening to false gods.

DAY OF ATONEMENT (YOM KIPPUR)

Held Tishri 10 (Sept – Oct)

This day was marked by fasting and great reverence. The high priest first made atonement for his own sins, then entered the most holy area to make animal sacrifices to atone for the sins of all the people. New Testament believers celebrated this as a victorious remembrance of Christ's shedding of His blood once and for all, and His resurrection which raises the believer up to new life in Christ.

FEAST OF TABERNACLES (BOOTHS OR INGATHERING)

Held Tishri 15 – 22 (Sept – Oct).

This feast commemorated the years of wandering in the wilderness by the Israelites before they occupied the Promised Land. To observe this, they were commanded to live in booths or temporary shelters for seven (7) days. It was a time to keep appointment with God, and rejoice in

God's glory. New Testament believers commemorated this time by 'camping out' in these booths, fellowshipping together, reading the Word together, sharing testimonies of God's goodness, and enjoying special times in God's presence with others or alone

FEAST OF DEDICATION (FESTIVAL OF LIGHTS/ HANUKKAH)

Started Chislev 25 for 8 days (Nov – Dec).

This feast celebrated the restoration of worship in the temple after its desecration by the pagan ruler Antiochus Epiphanes during the period of the Maccabees about 167 B.C. Jesus celebrated this festival in John10:22.

PURIM (LOTS)

Held Adar 14-15 (Feb – Mar).

This feast celebrated God's deliverance of the Hebrew people from the scheme of Haman to annihilate them when Esther was queen. This has always been an opportunity to thank God for His repeated deliverance from the hand of the enemy, and especially from situations that appear impossible. It reinforces that God is always looking out to find one of His children, backed up in a corner by the enemy, so He can show Himself strong on our behalf.

New Testament Believers did not celebrate Easter or Christmas. These holy-days were the invention of Constantine as He declared Christianity sanctioned by the state; merged the early church's commemoration of Christ's birth and death with pagan festivals; and suppressed the celebration of all festivals associated with the Jewish people.

What is God saying to YOU?

PURPOSE: LIVING WITH PASSION

My greatest passion and my purpose in life is to be a channel of the abundant life. God created us all to enjoy every moment of every day. However, joy is a gift that I embrace by casting all my cares on my Heavenly Father and by receiving His Shalom, His completeness. Only then am I able to model His Ways, make disciples by being a disciple, and demonstrate the following passions.

- ❖ Valuing myself

- ❖ Embracing abundant life

- ❖ Becoming a successful risk-taker

- ❖ Understanding self-reliance and responsibility

- ❖ Living free from stress and anxiety

- ❖ Operating from the realm of the Spirit 24/7

❖ Displaying the gifts and fruit of the spirit, and moving in the supernatural daily.

God gave me the above as some of the expressions of demonstrating Joshua 1:8.

This book of the Law shall not depart out of thy mouth, but thou shall meditate therein day and night that thou may observe to do according to all that is written therein; for then thou shall make thy way prosperous and then thou shall have good success. (Joshua 1:8 KJV)

What a great prescription for good success. Speak it continually, meditate on it continuously, and act on it continually. It is guaranteed.

RESTORATION - Available On Demand.

- Now is the time to believe for your miracle of restoration.

- Get out of the methods you are accustomed to.

- Move into God's patterns for this season, and into His new way of thinking.

  - ✓ Personally – in my life and my relationships

  - ✓ Corporately – as a church or organization

  - ✓ Territorially – immediate & wider geographical area to build and war for.

  - ✓ Generationally – We are living, to provide for the next generation.

- ❖ Restoring God's patterns, will bring restoration in these 4 dimensions to bring God's kingdom lifestyle on earth

- Watching – what God is doing and what the enemy is doing.

- Seeing – with the eyes of the Spirit, the truth that He leads us into.

- Bubbling - Affecting environments and people with joy, love, and peace.

- Speaking into future – Declaring His Kingdom Come, now, here on earth and watch it happen.

Whatever has gone down in the past can be restored according to God's perfect will. Once there is life, there is hope.

GOD'S PLAN FOR RELEASING FAVOR:

God's plan for releasing favor is in the spoken blessing. By doing this you put God's name on people and transform their lives.

We can remove curses of generations, financially, in relationships, health and release personal peace, love and joy.

The BLESSING :

- Study them
- Practice them
- Your child or student can move from straight F's to straight A's
- Fathers to bless children
- Parents to bless children
- Elders to bless younger
- Teachers and caregivers to bless those they care for.
- May the Lord bless you with……
- Say all the good that you want for yourself, and others.

Imparting blessings to impart supernatural spiritual and emotional bonding, will work for:

- Marriages

- Families

- And all relationships (see relationship hierarchy)

Satan's Plans - altering God's original intent through:

- **Cybernetics** – System of control and communications in living organisms which is being altered in the name of 'technological advances' to produce higher and bigger yields, BUT ends up destroying ecological balance.

- **Nanotechnology** – The engineering of functional systems at the molecular scale. It involves the manipulation and control of matter.

- **Genetic Engineering** – modification of an organism's genome as in adding new DNA to an organism – creates a dysfunctional organism.

- **Biotechnology** – Use of biological systems for technological application as in the manufacture of drugs and other chemicals (often without disclosing harmful side effects)

- **Fear Mongering** – The action of deliberately arousing public fear and alarm, by exaggerated and repetitive half-truths with the intent of distracting from workable solutions, and focusing on panic reactions.

- **Confusion** – creating a state of being bewildered and unclear, resulting in indecision and anxiety.

- **Cursing** – The expression of a thought that misfortune, evil, doom or other negative outcome befall a person, group or situation.

God's Plans - (Revert to God's original intent through speaking THE BLESSING. Lay hands on, and release the blessing over):

- Yourself

- Family

- Friends

- Enemies

- Associates

- Unborn children

- Circumstances

- Environments

- Communities

- Organizations

- Institutions – Schools, Hospitals, Places of Safety, Prisons, etc.,

- Nations

A BLESSING

The favor of the Lord IS upon you. You are blessed in spirit, soul and body, and experience the love of God 24/7 for the rest of your life.

Yeshua Ha'Mashiah Tsidkenu!

Practice speaking this blessing over everyone you encounter for a day, then a week, then a month then a year, and be an agent of releasing God's Blessing.

PHENOMENAL WOMEN & EXTRAORDINARY MEN

PHENOMENAL WOMEN

- Phenomenal Women choose extraordinary men as their husbands.

- Phenomenal women respect their men and confirm their headship

- Phenomenal Women lavish their men with love and keep their love tanks filled.

- Phenomenal Women raise sons and daughters to be extraordinary men and phenomenal women through God's love and grace

- Phenomenal Women live lives of focus according to God's plan

- Phenomenal Women love God with all their heart, soul and mind

- Phenomenal women live their truth with passion

EXTRAORDINARY MEN

- Extraordinary men maximize their potential through a relationship with God

- Extraordinary men protect, promote and provide for their woman and children

- Extraordinary men speak only words of affirmation and pray without ceasing

- Extraordinary men spend quality time with their spouses, family, coworkers and then others.

- Extraordinary men serve others in their actions

- Extraordinary men share their resources generously

- Extraordinary men give and receive expressions of loving, physical touch

HOW TO BREAK A CURSE

Jesus became a curse to break every curse on me.

We need to confess, repent and renounce every sin or generational sin.

Pray : I repent of any racism (see list above) in my life or the life of my family or generational history.

We repent on behalf of our government and we declare that their action should line up with the Word and purpose of God for our lives, our families, our communities, our organizations, and our nations.

Speak only what God says about me and others. You are not too old, too young or too far gone to receive a transformational touch from God.

SOME EFFECTIVE PRAYERS

I cancel every curse spoken over me, my family, my career, my church, my community, my nation or my ethnic group.

So Father I thank you that Jesus took himself the fullness of the curse we deserved so we could enjoy the fullness of His blessing.

Since your children have now confessed their sin before you; I now take on the authority that Jesus has given to His church and I cancel every demonic assignment and break every curse Satan has tried to afflict them with. In the name of Jesus, I now declare that the door for the curse is closed!

I thank God by faith that the curse is broken off of my life.

By faith I choose to move forward and enter the blessing this month and every day of my life in the future.

The NOW Word

God's WORD is always <u>given</u> in a particular context, to a specific person or grouping, at a specific time. It is always powerful, and sharper than any two-edged sword dividing between bone and marrow, soul and spirit. Although this is the genesis of all WORDS, (even if it is to all people for all time);   God's WORD is effective and relevant to all people at all times when they are ready to receive it.

God's WORD is only <u>received</u> when the hearer is ready to believe it, (trust in, cling to and rely on).

God's WORD is then <u>experienced</u> as a part of daily life when I meditate on, and act on and act out those things that are not, as if they were, until they become! In other words, the manifestation becomes a part of my reality long before the senses (see, hear, smell, taste, and touch) can experience it!

I have seen the following WORD, delivered in July 2014 in Antigua; received and experienced by numerous individuals, groups and nations in the past 24 months. What an awesome God! You may find it relevant to where you are now.

Father, these next three months you are going to infuse your people with a faith beyond ourselves. The Lord says, I will change the course of your praying, for you have prayed through your circumstances of your life and your family, you have prayed through the issues of your city (village) and state (parish), but I say to you I will now birth you into not just praying for your nation but praying for my kingdom to come in this land. I say to you this type of praying will begin to shake loose many things over the next three months, but I will shake those things that have been captured in other seasons, that have even compartmentalized your faith. I say, I will tear down walls within you that have been sealed up to keep your faith from synergizing and exploding! I say to you this day, you have returned to the new and now I will cause you to press through until the new fully manifests in the land you are living in.

Receive the commissioning for the mobilization into the next move of My kingdom in this land called Antigua, that will touch every nation that Antigua has ever touched.

Touch and agree!

Through: the ALWAYS BLESSED AND HIGHLY FAVOURED sherrillchong!!!

To: the Nation and the Body of Christ.

PS: Receive the sleep disorder of nightly revelation!

LETTER TO MOM

Below is one of my prized pieces of writing which was a direct download from the Throne Room. This one came down in response to my anger at myself for flying off at the handle again, and expressing myself in the most piercing, graphic and insensitive language. A trait I had rarely seen in my mother when she perceived that she had faced rejection. Later in life I had observed her marshal her stoicism, and re-channel those energies, into yet another learning pursuit.

So here I was, angry at myself and complaining to God, that I did it again; and it was my mother's fault because I had learnt it from her. My loving heavenly Father patiently listened to me vent, and when I was through, He asked me how old I was. I think I was approaching 50. He then asked, if I had a choice in the things I did or had a mind of my own; or if I was being controlled or directed by others. I bristled and answered that I did exactly what I wanted to do, and no one could tell me what to do. At this point, He reminded me that all my actions are preceded by a choice I had made to take that action, and that I always had a choice. I could choose the low road and run with how I felt, or I could choose the high road and soar above the challenges by focusing on the many beautiful characteristics that I had learned from my mother.

I wept and apologized, sat down and penned this letter to my mom, which I hand-delivered the next day. I shared this at her home-going service as she departed in a blaze of glory at age 93.

To My Darling, Dearest Mom,

This past weekend I just completed a presentation in a Parenting Empowerment symposium in Ocho Rios in ***"How to Discover and Develop the Genius in your Child."*** *It was a most enlightening and liberating experience for all the participants there, many of whom were 'delivered' from years of oppression by their families,* *the school system, the church and the society at large. As a result of this they were able to start to embrace God's promises that they can do all things through Christ; that they have been fearfully and wonderfully made; and that they are created unique individuals for a specific purpose. Then it all came together that I was in fact fulfilling my own purpose in life - that of helping God's children reach their full potential through Godly counsel.*

When I think of the thousands of persons that have been impacted by my life, I thank God for you, and bless you; for in spite of the many negative conditions which surrounded your childhood and later life, you turned every one into a learning experience and surmounted them to excel in every area that you participated in and everything that you touched. Today, when people express surprise at the many talents I have and the many accomplishments achieved, I usually inform them that God made us all with one or more geniuses (gifts, talents, abilities). While this is true, most person's natural love for learning is stifled first by their families, then choked to death by all the agents of the society as they carry out the enemy's diabolical plan to reverse what God says about us.

*I celebrate your spirit of excellence and enthusiasm for everything you did; your encouragement and motivation as you advised and directed each of us your children in the many escapades, endeavors and schemes we were continuously up to. Each of us can remember how you took time to help us with our homework, and showed interest in whatever **we** were interested in. You never displayed any type of favoritism nor compared us with each other, you always talked about our strengths, abilities and special talents.*

You showed us by example that we should always keep on learning, you were always studying, reading and improving yourself - no wonder they call me the perpetual student! I remember when in your 70's you were intent on learning Spanish, and in your 90's your insistence that Paulette, Carol and I join you in going through the new Jazz syllabus.

I thank you for passing on to me:

111

your creative genius in costume design giving rise to my boutique International Fashions by Elisa, and toy factory Sonshine Manufacturing Limited.

your tenacity in seeking solutions; remember my 'fallen ankles' and the special boots you had made by the shoemaker to straighten my feet (now you know why boots are my favorite shoes); and the ballet classes to strengthen my arches - even though the church would never approve (now my dance is used to minister in the church)

your passion for the performing arts - inspiring the formation of DESTINY Performing Arts Company which has revolutionized the lives of so many.

your love of teaching; especially those who were challenged - never giving up on the slow learners and those who didn't seem to have the 'gift'.

your love of learning at whatever age - I eventually started on my first degree in Theology at age 45 and am still pressing on toward my PhD now in my 50's.

your appreciation of a beautiful home and impeccable garden; do you remember my three years of studying interior design and my design company LISA LAKE LIMITED.

your ability to manage, organize, budget, and wear several hats at one time; giving rise to my organizational skills and entrepreneurial spirit.

the importance of living within our means and practicing sound financial principles leading to my financial independence and freedom from debt.

your love of travel, exploring new places and cultures, and the education that this exposure brought. I still remember that JOFFA tour we took in the 1960's from Miami through the southern States up to Washington. What an eye-opener!

the priority of serving God with all my heart and soul, and doing everything to the best of my ability to His honour and Glory.

I could go on and on because your impact and positive influences on me have permeated my whole life and will continue to steer my course. I know that Paulette and Donovan can share similar sentiments of your unselfish caring and unconditional love.

We love you dearly, and really appreciate all you have done for us and have been to us. As we rub shoulders with the world around us, we as your children are daily reminded how blessed, fortunate and exceptional we are to have had the upbringing that we had; and to have had a mother who nurtured, encouraged and celebrated our uniqueness and the geniuses God placed within us.

Thank you Mummy, for giving, and for teaching us to give. You are a one-in-a-million Super Mom.

I thank God for every remembrance of my dearest mother, and out of this experience, I have developed the habit of listing all the good qualities of those persons, who inadvertently display their carnal natures along this journey of continuous transition that we all travel. I have found that this lifts my spirit, aligns my soul, and detoxifies my body.

What a great way to live!!!

THE PROMISE PREVAILS FOR THE REJECTED

God is kind to the rejected! God specializes in rejects who have faith, who believe He is who He says He is, AND ARE WILLING TO FOLLOW HIM.

Whenever the enemy tries to oppress me, I simply scream for help; and my loving Father responds immediately, and usually reminds me of the millions that have gone before me, despised and rejected, yet they triumphed after rejection. I have listed a few of my favorites below. You can close your eyes and pick any of them, to be encouraged as you research their stories.

From the Biblical Account:

David, Joseph, Daniel, Boaz, Abraham, Moses, Esther, Ruth, Naomi, Rahab, Leah, Jabez, Abigail, Deborah, Elizabeth, Peter, Nicodemus, Eve, Jael, Keturah, Sarah.

One of the challenges of learning from biblical characters is that we are often unable to truly identify with them because of their portrayal as 'spiritual giants' or really evil persons. Many are unable to see the carnal natures of our heroes, and how the submission of these to God, enabled them to resist the devil in the events that are most lauded in the Word of God.

Every human being faces rejection (real or perceived). It is the enemy's number one 'wile' or deceitful strategy, often accompanied by fear of not being accepted by God or others. This feeling of not being enough in any given situation can only by removed by self-acceptance, that I am who God says I am.

What is God saying to YOU?

DISTRACTION VS. FOCUS

Distraction is one of the enemy's most effective tools. He can only achieve his objectives if he distracts me from the wonderful, easy, must-succeed plan that God has for my life.

Focus is the tool I must employ to remain as co-creator with God. The heavens belong to God, but the earth has been given to the sons of men. Along with this, I have been given all authority on earth. If I keep my focus on God's Love, God's Words, and God's Plan for me, (Submit to God); I can resist the enemy and he will flee from me.

Below I have listed the major areas in which the enemy often distracts us.

What is distracting you?	Get focused!
Health Challenges?	By Christ's suffering we were healed

What is distracting you?	Get focused!
Wealth? Can't make ends meet?	God promises to supply all our needs
Peace – worried or fearful?	God promises perpetual peace
Love – nobody really cares?	God's love is unconditional & lasting
Joy – life is stressful?	Receive Joy as you cast your cares on Him.

Focusing in the middle of every situation is where we have to guard against the distractions of the enemy. It is easy to start with a bang, when you look at God's promises and His intended end. But as we face the valleys, the obstacles, and the wilderness experiences that are an inevitable part of the middle passage; we will only get to God's expected end by focusing on the fact that the God who started a good work in each of us shall complete whatever He started.

So, don't think it is strange when you face different tests and fiery trials, remember that God will work out all things in your life according to His plan. Whenever the enemy tries to distract you during the challenging times, recognize that this is THE ONLY WAY that the enemy can prevent you from experiencing what God intended.

Whatever level of distraction you are having now, God invites you to refocus. This is something that I have to do very, very often. You can experience God's intended end for you... just keep focused.

Who are you distracting? Help them to focus!

Who is distracting you? Help them to focus!

I CAN LIVE A FOCUSED LIFE 24/7

1) Trust and obey immediately - in ALL areas of life!

2) Command the morning – Everyday!

3) Make a plan – then listen for God's voice to expand, delete, or adjust it

Command the morning today and every day, by declaring God's promises over yourself, and everything that concerns you. That is how, you can shake out the wickedness of passivity born of fear of loss of... whatever.

Command the morning today and be the prophetic voice of the body of Christ to speak into every circumstance of life.

+ Be a part of God's 'army' marching through this land.

+ Be an agent of joyful deliverance, and a channel of healing to the sick.

✦ Be an expression of everlasting joy and gladness in your relationships.

This is the part to be played, by all who believe, in this army.

God wants us to be constantly aware of the part we play in the 'army'. Be assured that we are victorious in every battle, if we remain in the battle to its end.

God has specifically positioned you to have influence for The Kingdom of God. He has called you; He has equipped you; and He has sent you. Go and take up your commission!

AN EXCELLENT SPIRIT – 12 Step Program

A 12-Step Program is one that has a desired goal of:

1) Rejuvenation of something that once existed;

2) Building up body, soul and/or spirit to achieve a new objective; and/or

3) The pursuit, overtaking and recovery of God's original intent.

- I declare I have an excellent spirit. – Declare God's Intent. My spirit is alive because of righteousness- I choose to come into right standing with God and Man (with God's help).

- I am the chosen of the Almighty.

- I hunger and thirst to be holy in love.

- I am adopted and predestined by Jesus Christ.

- I live in the secret place.

- My new man is alive to righteousness.

124

- I cry out for Grace according to the Divine Order of God.

- Let your Will, Plan, and Purpose unfold in Jamaica (and every other nation). With your anointing we overturn evil in our areas of influence and manifest the glory of God.

- Father, replenish us with Forgiveness, Truth and Grace.

- Restore us to Position and Purpose.

- I feast on your Spirit delighting in His fruit

- I adorn myself with the gifts of Your Anointing

SET FREE TO SOAR !!!

From as early as I can remember, I was always designing something. My earliest recollections are of dolls' clothing and accessories, followed by two doll's houses. My first house was designed and put together in a discarded bird aviary or pigeon coop. It had a concrete floor, was well furnished, was more than twice my height to the zinc roof and I had made steps to upstairs with discarded wooden boxes. My second 'house' had two stories, and a roof garden. This was converted from two crashed cars which were stored on top of each other in the back of our yard. I was about 5 years old at this time.

Since then, I have been researching and designing living spaces made from unconventional materials; and analyzing the effects of these spaces on personal development of the individual. The epitome of this passion came some 40 years later, in a stint as assistant to the Chairman of a National Housing organization, researching alternate building systems. I was so excited and prayed for an opening to impact the personal development of those occupying those living spaces; and immediately I was asked to help develop the management system to regulate the properties developed by that organization. Then I prayed: *Father, I want to work with the people, and show them how You can empower them to rise above their circumstances and thrive in, enjoy and care for a beautiful home.*

Within the year I had been contracted to train one person from each household that would receive a housing unit, in 8 communities over a five-year period. WOW! Now I needed to develop the curriculum to change the mindsets of those disenfranchised and downtrodden for generations, into persons empowered to become all that they were created to be!!! Only God could do that... He had been preparing me and all the materials for this task for years.

As the first community watched the beautiful structures rise from the ground, they also observed and participated in the transformation process of the course participants. This was a 3-month intensive program with workshops and deliverables on each topic. Set out below is the curriculum outline of *SET FREE TO SOAR!!!*

SET FREE TO SOAR!!!

A Transformational Personal Development Program

1) Getting to Know Yourselves: Physical Analysis, Genius Analysis, Temperament Analysis, Career Key.

2) Accepting and Becoming Yourselves: Dreams, Visions, and Love

3) Understanding and Utilizing the Laws of Growth

4) You and Your Environment – Interiors

5) You and Your Environment – Exteriors

6) Laws of Vision and Visual Poise

7) Laws of Word, Speech and Communication

8) Laws of Energy, and Grooming

9) Laws of Good and Evil, Wardrobe and Image

10) Laws of Abundance, Health and Happiness

11) Laws of Uniqueness, and Social Graces

12) Laws of Contribution, and Volunteerism

13) On Your Mark Get Set... and Life Development Plan

14) Planning the Events of Life

15) Graduation Exercise

Each and every one reading this article, has dreams that you are unable to bring to pass with your own resources. Agree with God, that if He has put those dreams into your spirit, He will bring them to pass. Just concentrate on seeking Him first in everything, and watch Him set you FREE TO SOAR!!!

SONSHINE MANUFACTURING

How would you like to work with an organization where your salary tripled in three years? Where 10% of gross profits were distributed equally to each employee each month? Where you could sing aloud through your day, and get up and dance to your favorite tune on the radio at any time if you felt like. Where 15 monthly employee awards were rotated, along with gifts of household appliances.

Where you were invited to a monthly birthday *bashment* (party/celebration), and could invite all your friends. Where you were encouraged and assisted in accessing whatever training you needed to achieve your future career goals. Where you were given a non-contributory health plan for you and your dependents. Where groceries including meats were procured by the company and passed on to staff at massive discounts.

Where daily devotions included special prayer and ministry to every person who desired it. Where each employee looked forward to coming to work each day, because it was an environment where they were affirmed, valued and loved.

Well, these were some of the benefits of working with *SONSHINE MANUFACTURING* where the light and love of God's Son was always shining.

Did it start off like that? Absolutely not! But God's word says that He will give you the desires of your heart. It also says that you have not because you ask not.

It all started when my Pastor asked my assistance in setting up a large 807 manufacturing operation as a community outreach project for the church. I requested a 9-month leave of absence, from the consultancy firm I was part of, which turned into four years. After 12 months of moving from one crisis to another, I screamed "HELP me Father, I am using all my best management techniques, and things keep getting worse. There must be a better way!"

That night, I was awakened at 3 a.m., and instructed to write. I reached for my ever present scratch pad, and wrote and wrote and wrote. I came to myself with a jolt, as the telephone rang at minutes after 8 a.m. because I failed to arrive at a TQM (Total Quality Management) seminar I had registered for at the Jamaica Pegasus Hotel.

OH, NO! This was supposed to be my opportunity to get solutions for the problems I was experiencing at the workplace. Then a quiet voice within me said: "Relax my child, you won't miss a thing, you will not be late!" So I took my time, and arrived at the seminar after the first break. I got my package, and scanned through the topics for the day, and the next few days. (It was to be a four-day seminar, and I had registered for day one only, to assess if this training would supply the answers I needed.) Well it was as If somebody had been looking over my shoulder as I wrote this morning. Not only was the analysis of my challenge outlined on this first day, but the topics for the solution were mirrored in the solutions and applications I had been given in my morning's 'vision'.

Needless to say, I did not stay for the other three days, saving thousands of dollars – it was a very, very expensive program; and redeeming three days of productive time.

I was instructed to do a four-page questionnaire for all employees, requesting details of their family relationships, training to date, ambition in life, what they are interested in and passionate about, and why did they apply for this job. I was to employ a university graduate with specialist training in running a factory sewn products line, to sit with one employee each day, and in the first half of each day, get the information for the questionnaire. During the second half of the day, she should train them in techniques that will so improve their productivity, that they will double their output, (and their income). It took just over three months to complete the exercise.

Next, every employee was enrolled in a training program that would move them towards their ultimate ambitions in life. The company assisted with fees and expenses. Those who were not enrolled in an external program were part of the Personal Development program which was run for all employees, in addition to on-the job training. As they doubled their output, they doubled their income and the company tripled its profits.

When you have an organization where employees are empowered to pursue their dreams, and take personal responsibility for their progress, you will have a happy, focused and progressive staff.

God has a plan for every entity, so find out His plan for your work community, and do your best to be a part of it.

What is God saying to YOU?

Write out in detail every dream and vision you have had for the organization or entity that you would like to start, have, or be a part of. Ask the Lord to refine it, expand it and bring it to pass.

Try your best to retain your joy through all the stress that the enemy will send, and keep or regain the love and peace through the trials and trauma... then share God's goodness with others through your own book.

GOD'S ORDER FOR THE CHURCH

God's order for the church – operating within the structure.

a) Built on Jesus Christ the chief cornerstone – Ephesians 2:20

b) The Five-fold Ministry Foundation:

- Evangelist

- Pastor

- Teacher

- Prophet

- Apostle

They equip the body for the work of the ministry through the development of the gifts and giftings.

c) Operating through the Fruit of the Spirit: LOVE - Joy, Peace, Patience, Kindness,

Goodness, Faithfulness, Humility and Self-control.

The believer's priority must be the development of the fruit of the spirit in our lives, so that we can properly administer or move in the giftings so bountifully lavished on us by God.

The Five Fold Ministers recognize and encourage the Body to exercise these gifts in the church and in their spheres of influence. Additionally they equip the Body to move in and use the following gifts:

Romans 12:6 – 8

- Exhortation
- Giving
- Ruling
- Mercy
- Teaching
- Ministry
- Prophecy

1 Cor. 12:7-11

- Word of wisdom

- Faith

- Word of Knowledge

- Healing

- Diverse Tongues

- Miracles

- Interpretation of tongues

- Prophecy

- Discerning of spirits

The above are to provide the framework out of which believers are to be empowered to bring heaven on earth and to express the glory of God in our everyday lives.

Our Spiritual, Psychological, and Physical lives were meant to be lived in an exemplary way by accepting and utilizing the many, many (free to us) gifts lavished on us by a benevolent, loving Father. Because most persons are ignorant of these gifts, they often spend their lives struggling to achieve the things that have already been paid for and are available just for the asking.

I will list without comment some of these gifts that I have benefitted from… just by asking.

Food, Rain, Physical Rest, Health, Sleep, All Things, Christ, Holy Spirit, Grace, Wisdom, Repentance, Faith, New Spirit, Peace, Spiritual Rest, Glory, Eternal Life, Living Water, and Love.

All good gifts come from God, cannot be bought or worked for, and are to be used for the expansion of the Kingdom (Rule) of God here on earth. As we focus on keeping the order within the church; it becomes easy to access all the things which are available. Then those outside will see the light emanating from our good works and come running to receive what their hearts are longing for.

Note: I have found that whenever I am unable to access any of God's promises, or am experiencing any negative emotion, there is a need to give and receive forgiveness – from God, from self, and/or from others.

What is God saying to YOU?

COVENANT

At creation God gave authority to man.

At salvation God/Jesus gave all authority to me.

Covenant cannot be broken. Covenant is a promise until death.

A contract can be broken. It is conditional – meaning that there are conditions which have consequences.

Covenant: God is always facing me and open to me.

I can choose to repent and accept His open arms.

I can also choose not to repent and allow the enemy to have his way.

My choice is to repent and accept God's open arms. But, these choices are like a recurring decimal; I have to make them many, many times a day, every day. God always presents His Way first, the enemy then comes with his plan to distract you from God's original intent.

My response to every plan of the enemy is:

God's love gives to everyone

God's word works in every situation

God's plan succeeds all the time and every time.

Help me, Jesus!   When I am weak, I will say I am strong.   When I am feeling poor, I will say I am rich; and when I am blinded by my own stupidity, I will say I can see…. by the Grace of God.

I believe God above what I see, hear, feel, taste or touch!

What is God saying to YOU?

PERSONAL & NATIONAL ANTHROPOLOGY

I have always been fascinated by the 'distinctives'; quirks, and peculiarities that I noticed, first within my immediate and extended family, then among those in the different communities with which I interacted, and paramount was the differences I saw in my childhood companions who were of other nationalities.

We all notice these things, and the usual response is laughter, disdain, or ridicule which are usually reactions of being uncomfortable with one's own 'distinctives'. At first, I went along with the crowd, but often wondered if I was also the object of those reactions. I did not like being laughed at! So, I asked God, why was everyone so different; and would I have to live my life trying to fit into a mold I did not particularly like, just to please others?

"Distinctives" – Differences that make individuals notable.

GOD'S ANSWER

My precious, precious child, Way back, before the start of time, I created you molecule by molecule, then I waited until the best time in history to assign you to parents, who would nurture you, an environment that you would thrive in, and a nation/ people group that you could help fulfil purpose. The path I planned for you is special, and a little different from everyone else... but do not be afraid, because I have equipped you with everything; remember, I said EVERYTHING you need to achieve MY PURPOSE with flying colours.

LISTEN FOR YOUR "ALL GOOD"

All things work together for good, to them that love God and to them that are called according to His purposes.

Whatever the enemy meant for evil, the Lord will turn around for good.

He (God) will do: Exceeding Abundantly Above All That I Could Ask or Think. (Referred to as 'the EAAAT-I-CAT thing' by me)

Above are three of my well worked affirmations that I have proven over, and over and over again. In fact, there is absolutely nothing negative from my past that has not worked for my good. They have turned out to be catalysts for blessing me, those connected to me in every way, (including my enemies); and impacting the world at large. God continues to do the EAAAT-I-CAT thing on everything I present to Him for His attention – as well as on those things that I am not even aware of!!! His miraculous intervention – EVERYTIME – has resulted in over-the-top blessing for me.

This is one of those broad spectrum fixes for whatever occurs, so be alert and listen out for your ALL GOOD.

GOD IS GOOD ALL THE TIME, AND ALL THE TIME GOD IS GOOD.

What is God saying to YOU?

THE CONCLUSION OF THE MATTER

GOD IS ALWAYS COMMUNICATING WITH EVERY ONE HE CREATED.

WE CAN ALL HEAR HIS VOICE. (Unless we have turned down the volume).

I MAKE A CHOICE, EVERY TIME I HEAR HIS VOICE TO OBEY OR DISOBEY.

My question to Him was, why do I disobey so often, when I know that You (God) are good all the time?

He very lovingly explained to me that my choices and decisions follow my focus.

If I focus on Christian media - audio, visual, print and artistic expressions - I will be encouraged, will gain knowledge of His relationship with others; but that is not what He is saying to me.

If I focus on my involvement in 'ministry' and doing greater works, I will acquire a false sense of accomplishment, pride, exhaustion and burn out. But that is not what He is saying to me.

If I focus on withdrawing from active service in my communities, analyzing and assessing what is wrong with them; I will develop another false sense of pride, and diminish God's intent for me to be an ameliorating or redemptive force within those entities. And that is not what He is saying to me.

So, what is He saying to me? I was frustrated with my repeated failures, and I longed for a formula for success.

God created me for relationship WITH HIM FIRST. He wanted someone like Himself to just be with, every moment of every day. Therefore, He created me in His image and likeness so we would be in sync and enjoy all the blessings of His creation. (Pause and think about that.)

HIs next words were: If you want the above, focus on this. That you may come to know me and experience the power of My resurrection in your life every day. Let this be the objective of how you structure your time; above listening and watching Christian media, above your involvement in ministry and church.

As this becomes our focus, we can truly enter into a realm where the experience of daily miracles will become our daily bread. We will become complete in Him. SHALOM!!

Let patience have its perfect work in you.

MY DESIRE STATEMENT FOR YOU

I pray that you will value, increase and protect your time with God; that your senses will always be attuned to His frequency; and that your daily journey will be enriched as you embrace His unconditional life-giving LOVE, experience His miraculous WORD at work in your life; and rest, relax and enjoy His awesome PLAN for your life.

I would really, really, appreciate your contacting me, and sharing how this book has stimulated you to hear God's voice more consistently for yourself. I would also like to hear the top three to seven topics from our table of contents that you would like more information on.

ABOUT DR SHERRILL CHONG

Dr. Sherrill Chong has been actively engaged in the leadership of the local church in the areas of Administration, Discipleship Training, and Evangelism (1985-1998 at Family Church on the Rock, Kingston, Jamaica and 1998 - 2006, at Holiness Christian Church, Bethune Avenue, Kingston, Jamaica).

Regarded as a fanatic in finding scripture to apply to every situation in life, she uses the Bible as her operations manual for every occasion in life including Family, Health, Relationships, Financial Freedom, Nation Building, and Personal Success.

She was married to successful businessman, the late Earl Chong who had a health and healing ministry of his own.

Dr. Chong's current passion is the training of Kingdom Shift Consultants in guiding individuals, families, communities and nations into God's Purpose for creating each one so that God's Kingdom may come on earth and His will be done on earth as it is in heaven.

Joshua 1:8

<u>Contact:</u>

Phone: (876) 819-3377
Email: dr.sherrill@yahoo.com
View: SCTV at http://reggaetoreggae.com

YOU CAN...EMPOWERMENT SERIES

You Can Empowerment Series is a radical approach to positive change. One that cannot fail because it is based on the principles of sowing and reaping, seedtime and harvest, on which all change – growth or deterioration – is based.

We will all reap what we sow... eventually, is an adage that most human beings hold to. However, this belief is somehow not borne out in most of our lifestyle practices, because of the cacophony of noises that somehow bombard our senses, drowning out our quiet, peaceful inner voice and tricking us to believe that we have no choice but to react immediately to the screams of crisis, the crashing sounds of violence and injustice; and the urgent cries of the helpless.

This Series attempts to look squarely at the present state of several aspects of personal, communal, and national life, which are experiencing crisis; that I have been exposed to. After there is analysis of how we got there, there must be acceptance of what is. THEN, instead of beating the dead horse by repeatedly bemoaning the current state of affairs; we individually, need to look within to see how each of us can be part of the solution. If I am not a part of the solution I am part of the problem. All solutions, chemical or problems, are made up of single components which supply what is needed for the intended end product. It is always a combination of different inputs, each supplying something different.

Because many of these situations have 'hit rock bottom' (that means most persons cannot imagine it getting any worse); only drastic measures will be able to resurrect the dead horse! Band-Aids won't do. A pain killer won't work. Even the wonder-working, detoxing, re-energizing effect of Jamaican Coconut Water will not bring the dead horse back to life. Only shock treatment, and open-heart surgery, while putting the patient on life support machinery, will restore life!!! In other words, only that which is necessary to regain and sustain life needs to be of concern... for the alternative is to remain dead. Attempts to fix the problem at the symptom stage by covering or getting rid of the evidence is counter-productive. Only when we address the issue at the core or foundational level will there be positive sustainable change.

The process being employed is the only certain way to achieve success in the process of change as laid down in the Operations Manual for Life; (The Bible) - Affirmative Imagery, Speech and Action (AISA)*. This is the positive outcome of sowing to the wind and reaping from the whirlwind, planting an acorn and finding shade under a huge Oak tree, and planting a single grain of corn and harvesting hundreds of seeds from multiple ears of corn. While this principle works splendidly for individual effort, the rewards proliferate when it is applied in family and community groupings; success requires the valuing of each contributor as essential to the process without assessing the quantity of contribution, only regarding the quality of the offering – "I have given my best". This brings to mind the words of a song called: I NEED YOU TO SURVIVE! I prefer to call it: *I Need You To THRIVE* (grow vigorously and prosper exponentially). It says in part,

I won't harm you with words of my mouth, I love you, I need you to survive ⋯

The application of the AISA Principle is the basis for all action, all growth, and all prosperity or demise. It is an automatic spiritual law which is constantly in action, working for or against us based on the <u>A</u>ffirmative that we <u>I</u>magine, what we <u>S</u>peak and the <u>A</u>ction we take. This is why we are encouraged in the Operations Manual to pull down every imagination that does not agree with what God says about us, and replace it with God's truth; speak only life into persons and situations; and expect, anticipate, and cling to, only the outcome God intended.

While my major concern is my beloved island home, Jamaica; my limited knowledge of world cultures and world politics seem to suggest that most other nations are facing similar challenges, in differing proportions. The principles for change outlined are universal, because they focus on the individual taking equal responsibility for the transformation, Yes! I said equal. Only when we embrace the truth that we are equal but different, can we each

158

recognize and accept our value to the whole... and celebrate that YOU CAN!!!...

Will you be a part?

*Copyright name to above process. While the principle is universal and open to use by everyone, the use of the name Affirmative Imagery, Speech, and Action (AISA) is owned by Dr. Sherrill Chong and available for use with acknowledgement of authorship.

Other Books In The Series (Unpublished)

- YOU CAN Be Happy 24/7

- YOU CAN Be Healthy, Wealthy And Wise

- YOU CAN Be Healed···Spirit, Soul & Body.

- YOU CAN Live A Life Of Praise And Worship.

- YOU CAN Choose To Love

- YOU CAN Alter Your Genes

- YOU CAN Enjoy All Of Life

- YOU CAN Find And Fulfill Your Purpose

- YOU CAN Have It All

- YOU CAN Have Wisdom

- YOU CAN Know Your Destiny

- YOU CAN Transform Jamaica

.

www.ingramcontent.com/pod-product-compliance
Lightning Source LLC
LaVergne TN
LVHW041220080426
835508LV00011B/1020